Boar and Family Books

Presents

# The Claw

Book 8

Cindy Gee and Gus Gee

Copyright 2024 Cindy Gee and Gus Gee

All rights reserved. No part of this book may be reproduced or transmitted in any form by any means, electronic or mechanical, including photocopying, recording or by any form information storage and retrieval system without permission in writing from the publisher.

Boar and Family Books- Madison WI

Paperback ISBN: 979-8-9895878-4-1

Hardcover ISBN: 979-8-9895878-5-8

Library of Congress Control Number: 2024902965

Title: *The Claw: Book 8*

Author: Gus Gee

Illustrated by: Cindy Gee

Paperback 2024

Hardcover 2024

Published in the United States by Boar and Family Books

This Boar's Family Book belongs to:

_____

_____

## DEDICATION

This book is dedicated to ALL of our breakfast club. We meet Sunday mornings to share a few laughs and enjoy each other's company. On the Sunday that this picture was taken the following were present.

Starting with the bottom left, moving up across the top, back down the right, then across the bottom are:

Gus, Cindy, Elisa, Jim, Nicole, Josh, Karen, Evelyn, Patrick, Elizabeth, Laurie, Kevin, Bill, Tracy, Linda, Betsy, Sara and Rachel.

"Let's go kids, we're going to be late" called Mom. "Dad is in the car waiting for us."

"Oh boy!" exclaimed Boar. "We are going to meet up with Mom and Dad's Sunday Breakfast Club to watch the game!

Junior commented "The part I loves best, is to play in the room with the claw and those machines that have spinning pictures."

At the restaurant the family greeted the others.  The Gee children got permission to go and play in the game room nearby

Junior wanted to play with the toys that were in the glass cage. She squeezed into the machine by climbing through the chute where the toys drop out. Junior wiggled her little green body up the track, into the glass enclosure. There she was amidst all the toys!

Oh no, another child came in to play the claw machine. They put a coin in the slot and positioned the claw over Junior. Junior not knowing what to do was very, very still and made believe she was a 'stiff' that is; she made believe she was one of the toys.

Horrified, Hardy and Boar stood in the corner and watched. They too acted as if they were 'stiffs,' that is stuffed toys, for they did not want to get noticed by the kid playing the claw machine.

Boar and Hardy watched as the child kept putting coins in the machine. Each time the claw would position closer to being over Junior the child would let go of the controls and the claw would drop.

Over and over the child tried to grab Junior with the claw, sometimes snagging Junior but she would fall out of the grip of the claw and into the toys below.  After many attempts, the child 'knew' the claw was in the exact position necessary to drop down and grab the green gecko, known to us as Junior.

Then it happened. The claw was in the precise, necessary spot to snare Junior. All the child had to do now, was to release the claw.

The child, sensing victory, looked down at the controls, took a deep breath. While still looking down the child released the controls and dropped the claw!

At this exact moment Junior noticed that the child had looked away from her and down at the controls. Junior quickly, but quietly, slide out from under the claw and kicked the nearby stuffed banana in the place where she had just been standing.

The claw, released, came dropping down faster and faster and fell upon the banana. When the claw closed and raised, the banana, not Junior, was in its grasp.

The claw raised with the banana and moved to drop the prize down the chute. Just then the banana slid out of the claw and fell on top of Junior! Frantic the child reached into its pockets searching for more coins.

Then a hush fell upon the room.  The child's parent came and the two left the room.  "Whew!" sighed Hardy, Boar and Junior.  "That was close" said Junior from inside the glass enclosure.

Boar motioned to Junior and said "Come on out." Junior looked around but could not find where she had entered the machine. The child had mixed the stuffed toys up and around. Junior cried out "Boar, I'm lost!."

Hardy shouted "I'm going to go get Mom or Dad to help." "No! Please! Do NOT do that!" pleaded Junior. "Don't tell Mom and Dad!"

Junior looked at Boar who had moved to the front of the machine. Luckily, this just so happened to be the place where the toys drop from, and the way Junior had climbed in. Junior cried out in glee "I know where the opening is Boar! I see it! I am coming out!"

Junior wiggled her way out of the machine, the same way she had climbed in.  When Junior was out of the machine she hugged Boar and Hardy.  The three looked at each other and laughed.  "That was close" said Hardy.

"I'm never doing that again," promised Junior. "Let's go see Mom and Dad and get some hugs." The three siblings did just that.

www.ingramcontent.com/pod-product-compliance
Lightning Source LLC
LaVergne TN
LVHW070536070526
838199LV00075B/6790